Thoughts Of A Melanin Women

Robdreka Simmons

BookLeaf Publishing
India | USA | UK

Presentation by *BookLeaf Publishing*

Web: www.bookleafpub.com

E-mail: info@bookleafpub.com

ISBN: 9789360944421

First edition 2024

ACKNOWLEDGEMENT

I first have to acknowledge God for bringing me this far and placing all that he placed inside me. Thank you to those who help support me in publishing my first and now second book. Thank you to all those who believed in me. Thank you to my parents (Robert Simmons and Rosie Simmons) as well as my spiritual parents (Ruben Lewis and Linda Lewis) for bringing me up in the right way. The knowledge you all have instilled inside me will forever be with me. Thank you to Girls Write The World for helping me step out of my comfort zone to write.

Significance Of An Angel

(Dedicated To Angel, April 1,2003-November 8,2022)

April 1st, 2003 is the day you were birth,
November 8, 2022 is the day you died.
Yet, I didn't get to say a single goodbye,
Sometimes I ask myself if I could've done it differently like,
Apologize and tell you the fallout is petty, but yet you were spoiled and stubborn so it wouldn't have worked.
There's a few things I wished I could say to you like…
I love you and wish I had one more chance with you.
Friends come and go but never thought when you left you weren't coming back.
Girl just know me and your best friend still holding on.
I love you like a sister but it was time for you to fly your wings.
I mean I don't think it was a coincidence your name was significant because your name told us who you are.

I guess you came into this world to be a grace
unto us.
Angel became an angel, just soar your wings
boo.
& I ain't grieving because this is a celebration
everytime your day comes around.
Just tell me one thing: can you see my granddad
with you too.
He left a day before my birthday in 2018 without
a goodbye too.
Just know I love y'all.
Life will never be the same.

This Is Why I Love You

Why I love u?
I ask myself a million times...
My heart is flooded with emotions for u.
Sometimes it's hard to draw away from u.
My heart is with u even when u think it's not.
This is why I love u...
Because when I was at my lowest, u accepted
me fully.
You loved me the most when I was learning
myself again.
I'm still learning how to be myself again but u
help me become that person more each day..
I lost myself & u help me find her.
This is Why I love u...
I'm so confused, my heart is heavy.
Which one I want, which one I choose.
Leave or stay, either way I lose so this is why...
Exactly why I love u because u love me most
beautiful.
It's time we settle down & understand to stop all
the bs & playing.
Why I love u, I ask myself.
This is why I love u,
I don't know why nah that's a lie.

I love u because u comfort me and reassure me
that you're the one for me.
The one to hold me,
The one who chose me.
Wouldn't misuse me nor abuse me.
I give u my heart & you only soothe me.
Cherish this heart of mines like a gem, cause it's
a diamond in the rough.
Made & built from the pressure & pain
This is why I love you

Dear Younger Self

(this is dedicated to the younger you)
You ever have those talks with yourself,
The kind when you say everything you wish
someone else would say to you.
Dear Me,
I love you & I miss you dearly.
THey robbed you blind took away your
innocence before you knew how to speak.
Thank you, for staying so quiet in every room
you went into.
That helped you see everything around you
better.
Thank you, for having my back through
whatever.
Forgive them people who hurt you, broke you,
abused you.
They didn't know who you were, they never saw
the light within you.
Know that every story has a purpose,
& everything that glitters ain't gold.
Know that you're a true Gem, diamond in the
rough.
Watch who you trust & the company you keep.
Watch who you try to build with. Don't let
everybody eat with you.

Don't hold on to grudges because they turn into illness & addictions.

Be patient, don't rush your youth cause you're going to wish you could go back.

Not everybody is out to hurt so make sure you're healing.

Make sure you put God first and find out who you are.

Make sure you listen to that wisdom them older people dropping, it could probably help you.

Most importantly know it's okay to be alone, love yourself.

I also want you to know to focus on building your wealth, you'll never get another chance at life so don't let them rob you from setting up life for yourself.

Your Pillar Of Rest

Sometimes I want to give it my all, but I may be
scared to fully let down my guard.
When I caress you my heart is saying to you:
"Let me be your Comfort, the reason you smile,
Sometimes I have trouble showing affection but
people in the past didn't know how to cherish it.
For you though I'll risk it all, let me be your
pillar of rest.
Even through the pain, you can trust in me.
After a long day, when the rest of the world
stresses you out, baby you have a friend in me.
Leave it all at the door, cause with me you don't
have to worry.
When they ask me what I see in you, I say I see
a King within.
And even though I had practice to get right,
I still ask God "prepare me to be the best woman
I can be for him."
I mean you're a king so you'll be honored by
me.
Let me be the one to polish your crown, I'll be
your pillar of rest boo."

Addiction To The Struggle

One of the hardest lessons to learn is to forgive.
They teach us everything that doesn't pertain to
life, but how about teaching us how to deal with
pain.
Teach me how to control my mental state,
cause I be lashing out.
They said "love would be dangerous and come
with problems."
But how can you move on without letting go and
forgiving?
You'll forever stay stuck with that burden and
extra baggage, huh
& let's talk about family fucking family that
ain't right.
When I look at what I grew up with it was
nothing,
but seeing who I could become made me want to
be better though.
I can't move on and not live in the past of what
happened if I don't let it go.
I know it seems like everybody is sleeping on
you too,
 But as long as you know there's a gift in you.
Just got to hustle the best way you know how
cause there ain't no handouts in the struggle.

From the people standing on the blocks and
corners some people will never know.
Trying to upgrade your status so you won't be
categorized in the same area of those you've
grown up with.
I don't want to be seen as someone who's not.
 The struggle only made me better though,
It's something about seeing what you don't want
to become that'll drive you to insanity if you
don't get something different than what you're
living in.
Some people want to stay stuck. I would rather
free myself up.
The thing about the crabs in the bucket is that
they'd rather see you suffer with them than see
you make it out.
I guess they're just addicted to the struggle huh.
But yet you never know if you'd even make
either though, cause you used every ticket you
had to make it out.

Dear melanated Man

Dear Melanated Man,
You so sexy, ohh you blessed.
Dear Black Man,
I love you, they try to suppress you but let me
uplift you.
Dear Melanated Man,
I see you, you're so great within cause you're
the closest thing on earth that I can see as god.
Dear Black Man,
You're worthy , so when the rest of the world
beat you down,
know that it's some queens out here looking to
let you wear your crown.
I'm talking about some real queens that'll go to
war for you.
The ones who willingly would lay there and
birth every generation for you if they could.
The queens who know how to be your peace
when the whole world is against you.
The ones who knows your value as a black man
and want to help you heal.
Dear Melanated Man,
Who hurt you baby, it's time to put that pain to
rest.
Lay here with me and I'll let God do the rest.

Dear Black Man,

You're special, you're a king and I honor every part of you.

And when the whole world is against you, I'll be here every way with you.

I'll get on my knees in prayer and cry out for you.

I'll take your house and create a home for you.

I'll sacrifice my life to bring another life in this world for you.

And my only hope is that God blesses you.

Through it all, I'll only submit to you.

I'll make you proud to say "that's my lady, she's a queen for real."

Letter To My Mother & Father

Thank you, for the faith you both have placed in me.

Thank you, for not being perfect so I can learn how to manage in this world alone.

Because of you I will know what love looks like, it's the opposite of what I've seen from your marriage.

Because of you I will know how to be independent & survive on my own,

I didn't get to be a child as a child cause I had to survive.

My advice to the both of you would be to forgive because the burdens you held was taken out on us.

Mama thought she knew what she was doing, she took us from daddy & said " you will never see him again."

It hurt me the worst though when daddy didn't come for me,

I guess I held that against you all these years, I'm sorry.

Maybe my anger towards you made me bitter towards you,

Maybe it's my anger against men.

See, daddy when you weren't around I cried out
in hurt for you.
So many times I was molested or touched.
I walked around in discomfort for so long &
nobody knowed what was really going on.
For so long I suffered in my silence,
Depression became my best friend & worst
enemy in the same minutes.
All my life it was one parent without the other,
I held on to the abandonment of not having my
parents' love.
Tough love's not real love when you're already a
broken child.
All the things my dad said were wrong with me I
began to believe.
I became exactly what he said every word
absorbed me.
I tried to let go of the hurt I held within but you
never acknowledge the hurt you caused me.
My mother did but daddy didn't.
I was once daddy's little girl,
But daddy's little girl was no longer the same
little girl with her innocence stolen.
Daddy's little girl had seen the world at it's
worst & knows it for what it is.
Daddy's little girl became her mother,
I remember times I watched my mother get
abused by other men & I thought daddy
would've never done that.

I told myself I will never go through the same as
my mother,
so anytime I get in an abusive relationship I'm
quick to run.
Mama & daddy taught me how to survive
through the struggle cause I struggled all my
life,
It was never comfortable for me.
I forgive you all for the pain I had to deal with
alone while missing your presence.
Thank you, for not being perfect parents.

A Healing King

My love is so deep your heart will feel it a mile
away.
My love is so deep that when your heart hurts,
mines hurt too.
God can only protect you…
His heart shall be safe within me.
See when I see a king who's broken I alway
want to fix whatever's within.
I challenge their ability to be anything different
than a king.
Cause when you're with me you're going to
know exactly who you're supposed to be.
So when you hear me call you king don't doubt
that you're really that indeed.
I look deep within so I can cleanse the things
you fight within.
I'm one of those who really believe in what a
man can be.
I won't speak against your mind or pride,
because that'll make you feel less than a king.
I cry out for healing to take hostage of you.
I like the person you become when I'm right
next to you & I know you wonder what it is I
think of you.

To me you're golden, something much different
than what you may feel.
King I believe in you, I know you can heal every
broken thing within & heal yourself as well.
I accept your flaws because we all have them,
I'm not here to tear you down so I do my best to
make you feel uplifted.
I'll speak to your mind as if it was my own.
Healing is a process that I myself even have to
realize is a process that's precious.
So take your time , all the time you need to heal
within.
My prayer for you is that you heal from the
things you don't talk about.
-To All The Healing Kings

What It Means To Be Incarcerated…

I lost the LOML to the institution,
Incarceration to me means taking a black away
from his family & women.
Take him out the streets before he could get
anything established.
Don't let him build a legacy or produce any
children.
The less production he builds,
the better chance we'll have at killing their
population.
We only want you to fail so we'll tear you down
if you don't sell your soul.
We'll say "One Nation under God" but we don't
even honor the God of your nation.
We took you away from your home so your
children won't have you around,
You won't have the resources or knowledge your
ancestors passed down through generations.
We'll beat you & change your identity so you'll
forever be searching for yourself.
We've been incarcerating you all your lives, but
now you make it easy to.
We start hood beef so you can have a reason to
kill each other.

I lost my uncle to the institution,
Incarceration to me means he'll die in prison.
Let your last memory of me be the moment you
seen me before the judge.
I'll never forget everyone who rehearsed these
words "sorry I let them take me away from
you."
We can't choose anyone's path for them,
But I feel we can teach our sons so they'll never
have to face the world alone.
Cause incarceration to me means watching your
sons die while they're young.

Life

Dear life,
You hurt me, but I love you anyways for just
putting up with me.
I've been broken over & over but you never
cease to amaze me.
I needed the trails you put me through,
I had to run that race so I could be prepared for
the war.
I love you for keeping me all this time.
I'll be okay & just fine one day these days will
get better.
I must be one hella of a soldier all these battles
I'm fighting.
It's time I put down the liquor & deal with my
hear.
I said pick up my heart so I can finally deal with
my insanity.
I will find peace,
If I was to leave tell me who would notice
enough to even miss me.
When I write don't think it means I'm not okay,
I just had to make room to acknowledge the
trauma I once felt.
I so deeply used to feel so not okay.

I had to replace my pain with pen & paper so I
wouldn't hear them demons telling me to end it
Anxiety became my best friend & my worst
enemy in the same minute.
When my therapist would ask I would never tell
them how I felt completely.
If only I could tell you how many times I sat up
crying to God wishing he could refill me.
Hell, just hear me.
God I don't think you feel me.
Dear life,
I'm busy, busy dealing with the trauma you
placed within me.
They didn't tell me that healing wouldn't be easy.
I decided to get up though & deal with my
demons.
Me & my demons don't get along it's always a
fight continuously.
I choose to be free from all my unshattered
dreams.
Those dreams will one day be for me,
Cause I'm always winning no matter what it's
seeming.
Dear Life,
I'm winning this game you played so unfair.
Now I'm smiling.
I know you hate to see I'm finally healing &
letting go of your minions.

Your minions has forever tormented me but now
it's time I live for me to be free from the curses
you placed on me.
Every curse has been broken.

To The Man Who Doesn't Know where My Heart is

I wish you knew how I felt about you or do you know how I feel but just don't know how to accept the love being given to you…
 I know you've been through a lot & I have too but I'm willing to put my guard down for you.
I've never been so crazy about a man the way I am about you.
 I want to settle down with you but I'm scared of being hurt again even though I'm scared I'm still willing to try for you.
I think about you so much & it's like I can't believe I have a man like you. Don't change on me, I don't care what you do as long as you don't change on me & continue to pursue me.
Make me happy & I promise to do my best to do the exact same.
I love you & don't know how this happened. Sometimes we could ask God for something & we'll get it & not know it's really what we asked for because we're in doubt that he's really done that for us.
We can mess up something good by pushing it away not knowing it's exactly what we asked for.

God, I love you & I promise I questioned myself
a million times if I actually loved you cause It
seemed so sudden.
I don't want to bring you no bad news, forever
giving you good news. Treat you like a king
cause I ain't never had a man that I saw so much
value in.
If nobody else ever told you this my love you're
special & you're different. You don't have to
keep looking because I'm right here I can be
whatever you want or need me to be for you.
 I honor your role as a man in my life,
Most women don't know how to treat or handle a
man like you but I do.
 I see grace when I look at you.
You're searching for an answer in this world.
Well, here is the answer. You've been asking for
a second chance at life thinking you haven't
gotten it right but it's not you that didn't get it.
Your self conscious can be your worst enemy I
would know cause it can be mine too.
 Always second guessing if something could be
real but I promise you this is.
 So if you were looking for a sign here it is, I'm
right here.
 What you're gonna do with the gift that you
were given your most prized possession, your
ruby.
Far more precious than gold.

When this message finds the person it's for you
will know that God has favor to look upon you
with his grace & give you your chance so get it
right & don't look back at the past.
 Let's move forward my baby cause you're now
on the winning team.
 I don't know who this is for just yet but I'll
know whenever I know & you will receive it.
So just know I love you king.

Salt Of Earth

My favorite wine is Salt of the Earth,
I like to sit back & sip thinking about how we're
the salt of the earth.
How did we get this bad?
Our communities are falling, get nobody is
saying anything.
& I could've sworn the sky was weeping for the
mercy to come upon a senseless nation.
A divided nation upon our own race,
Only a few waking up, we need to hurry the
pace.
We a dying race, so hurry the pace.
I'm crying for my race that's senseless to
knowledge,
Cause see we're the salt of the earth our skin is
connected & absorbs the sun.
We are so connected to the earth, our hair is
resemblance of a tree.
Some real shift shapers have stood on earth
before me,
The wind just whispered sweet melodies to me
while the sun gave me a kiss.
I looked at the clouds as heaven opened for me.

The birds sing to me " you belong with the most
high angelic King, the one who is he who's spirit
is within me.
When I rock a style that speaks culture, I know
that I'm connected to who I am.
I shed light in every room I step into,
Cause I'm salt who touches the earth.
I don't look back because those who look back
turn into a pillar of salt.
I know who I am salt of the earth, dust particles
put together & molded me.
& When I leave, I'll leave the way I came breath
of a spirit placed in flesh.
There's nothing broken about me no more I got
rid of who I thought I was & became salt.
I can heal cancer in the bones with one touch.
Don't play with me and my abilities,
I've suffered burdens so gracefully to get this
purpose in me.
The difference between me & them is I heal
through touch, they heal through drugs.
I'm salt of the earth, we're salt of the earth.
& I can only say God is within me because I've
realized who I am to the earth.

June 5, 2018

I'll never forget the phone call I received a day
before my birthday in 2018,
It was so hurtful & I didn't want to believe the
words.
I hung up the phone on my sister trying to
suppress that pain swelling up from the emotion
of the news I was hearing.
To be honest until I heard her say that I wasn't
even listening.
I loved you so much & my best friend was no
longer with me.
Who do I go to & how can I find something to
fill the emptiness of the presence I'm missing?
My grand daddy is missing, his flesh was
lifeless.
He has exited his temple, so where did his soul
go?
Where did you go, why did you leave me?
I guess God was trying to warn me because a
few days before you left me I had a vision.
A vision that you would leave me & how
everything in life was changing.
I prayed he wouldn't take you from me cause
you were so healthy.

They say you died of natural causes, but really
you were tired of this old life you had been
given.
I'm letting go now, I held on to you so long
before I could though.
I love you grand dad & I know God had better
for you.

Different Me

I'm at the point where I'm tired of giving out
more than I'm being given.
Giving out love more than I receive I.
Caring for people more than they'll ever care
about me.
The me now is winning, I became so different.
The old me would've fell for those wack lines
you spitting,
The new me knows better & telling myself "girl
get some sense."
The old me was afraid to let go or say no,
New me saying "you got to go."
The old me cared about people's opinion,
Now I ain't even listening, lol.
If I ever needed a validation of who I should be
then let it come from he that is HE! big G not
the lil one.
Old me showed up for everyone but herself,
The new me will never lose myself for someone
else.
The old me had knowledge without wisdom to
guide it,
The new me has grace, respect, wisdom, and
knowledge so no I won't dare settle for less.
So, Excuse me for knowing that I have worth.

If I tend to distance myself just know at one
point of time I was so used to being alone
standing on my own.
My circumstances are what made me strong,
A different me progresses daily.
I'm not a fool slaved to this world but free…
Free indeed.

Toxic Therapy Part 1

When I tell people "I don't believe in religion,"
they think I'm not connected to God .
But I don't remember God saying in order to
build a relationship with him,
I have to identify as a certain religion.
As much as I talk to God & see him perform in
my life I'd like to think I'm very favored.
I mean how you think I got this knowledge of
how to move through life.
& how can I know a good man when I get one if
I've never seen my dad be an example of that to
me.
I got brothers but they barely were around to
teach me.
I got this one brother though that set an example
for me, so I try to look for him in men.
But men don't come like that today.
& my mind is so ventful that sticking to one
topic in this poem will just not be a gateway for
me.
Cause you see this is my toxic therapy, my
thoughts so elevated I think of everything.
& sometimes I think they don't believe in, hm
the family I got.

Some may say the words I speak are dark but
nah,
This is real life for me.
As i write I speak my story, see I ain't here to
impress nobody my life ain't flawless you see.
Nobody has a perfect story but some can take
there's better than others,
But then there's me who was a broken mess
through each & every test.
I begged God to complete me & heal me.
Then next thing I knew another language of
tongue flowed through me so graciously.
I'll never forget that day you see, he came to
rescue me.
Some of you who don't believe will never know
the feeling of overflow that set down so heavy
on me, man.
It was so amazing you see, I kept running back
again & again for that feeling of covering.
My once toxic therapy became not so toxic
therapy.
I was able to live & breathe again.
Nobody but God himself knew the burdens of
hurt & depression that captivated me.

Toxic Therapy Part 2

I've tried to commit suicide on several occasions
you see.
Man, how he wouldn't let life fade away from
me from the time I was a baby laying there
going "code blue."
Trauma from molestation only at the age of 2
took away everything.
I don't tell my story for pity you see, but to be
healed & complete.
& would you believe me if I told you I've
experienced molestation or even being touched
on so many occasions.
Not only have they done it to me but every
female in my family has a story you see.
But they say "sweep it under the rug" "whatever
goes on in this house stays in this house."
God told me to speak up though you see, cause
after being silent about where these scars on my
body come from for so long, you have an
everyday reminded of the pain you've endured.
You'll never get an apology so you have to heal
either way.
I choose to deal with my pain & not let it hold
me hostage again.

Toxic Therapy Part 3

What about the times no one was there when
you & your sister were homeless.
& sometimes I feel like my dad could've fought
for us not to be taken away from him when him
& mama separated,
Maybe we wouldn't have to endure some of the
pain we did.
"Why didn't you come for me?"
Now I'm bitterly bruised.
When I became an adult I looked for love in so
many places before my cup was refilled.
So you can't tell me I wasn't blessed & highly
favored all the times I watched my mom get beat
on by another man.
Daddy wasn't there to rescue me from that man
harming me & my sister.
By the time he came back around to get me it
was too late, depression had already taken over
me.
Imagine suffering at home then getting bullied at
school because you're the new girl & wasn't
used to the country life.
I just want to go back home to the southside of
Greenville, Ms where I've always been.
The kids at school are right. I don't belong here.

I've had to heal & forgive so many people but
no apology was given to me.
Forgive me if this therapy is too deep for you.
But I'm just asking someone to listen to my not
so toxic therapy.
My whole life I've tried to be who everyone else
told me to be.
But now I'm me & living for me & don't care
about any opinion of me.
That man who saved me so mercifully is the
only approval I need.

Generations Of Hope

To the little black girl & boy who needs a
purpose, I see you.
Dark days, I mean those dark clouds are heavy.
I see you crying in the dark wishing you had
someone to give you wisdom.
You see, nowadays kids don't have the wisdom
we used to.
What happened to the older people that cared
about the minds of the young people.
Their being captivated everyday, I see you.
Somebody help us, yet we grown folks not
listening to what's destroying these babies when
they try to talk about it.
How many black boys have you seen die in your
community, whew.
Sometimes I have to let out the air to breathe
cause excuse my language but this shit gets
heavy.
See me I grew up having proper respect,
 you see grown people talking… you be quiet &
mind your business.
But nowadays these children talk slicker than
some butter.
& we can't blame them if that's all they seen,
Some barely grew up without a mother or father.

I don't see no one else venting about this
problem but I am.
& grandmama dying so how can we pass on the
recipe for biscuits.
Now it's a gift if you get to see my age,
Because 21 is an age most never get to see.
Then some kids looking older than me let's talk
about why,
They don't know how to express themselves so
they turn to drugs & alcohol.
They don't care anyways just another black boy
who won't rise as a king,
Another black girl who doesn't even know she's
a queen.
Someone has to help these babies for our nation
become non-existent.

To The Man I Lost Forever

(Dedicated to the woman who lost a man to
death or incarceration, Keep your head up
boo!!!)
Thank you,
Because of you I'll never settle for less because
that's what you told me.
I'll never forget when you called me & told me
that.
You used to say I was the only thing in your life
that's pure,
Tell me what Did you mean by that?
I loved so deeply, I loved you so hard & I
figured I'll heal by now but every time a man
breaks my heart I think
Man, he'll never do that to me,
But I seem to forgot you were the one who
actually did something to hurt me.
Even when you would hurt me though you knew
how to reassure me and console me.
You set an explain for me of what a man should
be.
I think constantly that you said "never settle for
less than what you deserve because you deserve
so much,"

Yet it took you to be away from me caged like
an animal for you to realize that.
& Everything I told you it took your situation for
you to realize all I was saying to you.
I tried to warn so many times so you wouldn't
ever leave me,
I remember I always told you I never want to
lose you to these streets or to other things.
But you let them take you away from me,
How do you do that?
How could you be so selfish with your life
knowing the attachments that I had with you.
I mean I thought I was made for you,
 the crazy thing is I never really got over you.
It's like you been gone forever,
I remember the day you got locked up in
December.
You promise you were to come back & take me
on a date.
We were talking about forever, we were
supposed to be getting married.
My advice to any women if you got a man that's
in the streets be prepared for whatever,
I lost mine to the cells soon as he was thinking
about changing.
But maybe me & God knew if he didn't sit him
down he would get right back in them same
streets he done lost his people to.

To be honest I didn't know what I'm supposed to
do without you,
Had to learn how to readjust & live without you.
I know I said forever & always,
 but tell me how forever will last if it doesn't last
too long these days.
I know we always said loyalty over love but I'm
desperate without you out here, sad to say.
I figured out you're one of my strengths and
weaknesses.
I'm always so used to being strong but I'm not
strong always.
You taught me so much as a man that I didn't
know before,
Nobody else built me the way you did.
If it wasn't for me being with you I probably
wouldn't have found God again, because most of
the prayers I prayed went like
"Dear God, protect him."
& I remember one night I had a dream then
found out he really protected you like he did in
the dream.
See we were connected, neither of us understood
it but we knew it was something different.
 I mean you carried the book of Proverbs &
Psalms everywhere with you.
You wore the serenity prayer and held it so
dearly,

It made me wonder how can a man who knew he
was protected by God still choose the street so
much.
You could've known it's not too many chances
he'll give you,
But hey, You can't help what your environment
adapted you to.
It was something you were so used to.
& You knew when I was tired from life to the
point everytime you would take your hand under
my chin, lift up my head then hug me with
comfort.
You always knew just what to do, gotta admit
you were so smooth cause nothing in the world
you could do wrong could make me feel any
different about you.
Cause I knew the real you, I knew the king in
you nobody else knew.
I knew your dreams and visions too.
You told me to move on with my life, but God
knows I would wait for you.
& I wish we could do it over again with the
experience of our ups & downs now.

My Skin: Melanin

I love to look at the different shades of brown.
It's like the beautiful touch from the sun kisses
has just melted into a golden pot of clay.
I mean I know you ain't scared of a little
chocolate right.
I don't know about y'all but I love me a little
chocolate kiss or honey baby shea butter is
moist.
Feeling of essence as you stroll through the
streets.
Don't ever let them make you feel ashamed of
the skin you're in.
See they don't know your roots got power and
strength.
That hair ain't nappy, it's kinky, full of strength.
You can tie and twist and turn it still it'll hold
just like a rope.
So nah, I don't get offended when they tell me "
your hair looks like yarn or rope"
Well, at least it has a natural bounce.
See the pigment of my skin has grace me and
shape me into some type of art.
My hair flows as free as a stanza in a poem.
My skin is as smooth as the lyrics of your
favorite rapper.

My skin is popping, I love my skin.
If you regret being black then you need to look
within, we come from a long heritage of royalty.
Your skin looks like royalty even,
that's that rich bronze.
Golden and chosen.
Why you think they wanted so badly to abuse it?

I Write Because

I write because there's a soul who needs to hear it.
I write because my people live in oppression.
I write because I am not my trauma.
I write because at one point I was too quiet & didn't have a voice to express in this world.
I write because my heart is always weeping for the generations & I can't dare to be silent about it.
I write because there's a little girl who's venting to me in a corner not knowing what to do with her life but ending it.
I write because I have to feed the nation of babies growing up after me.
I write because my belly is full & I can't hold on to the words that overload it.
I write because one day I noticed how low my vibrations were low & I had to be so much greater,
Without the envy, anger, and feelings that held me back.
I write because I came from a family of dysfunction so I had to break these curses.
I write because I keep growing on a daily basis.

I write because I'm not who I used to be but
realized I'm a queen.
I write because I am ancient & come from
royalty.
I write because I'm healing to birth a nation of
unbroken children.
I write because these scars ain't come from just
chilling my whole life.
I write because I actually went through it.
I write because I was that little girl who was
abused, bruised and broken.
I write, I write because I got some people who
need uplifting, stuck in a system that doesn't care
if they make it.
I write because I know that somebody will be
touched by it.
I write because I'm blessed, I write because
these hands are gifted.
I write because I'm tired of being so damn
strong…
I write because my life ain't golden but I
promise you I ain't folding.
I write because I've been beautifully broken to
become a queen.
I write because I now know the purpose to be
chosen or to be loved by yourself more than you
can love another.

www.ingramcontent.com/pod-product-compliance
Lightning Source LLC
LaVergne TN
LVHW041241200726
843507LV00013B/2765